Poems by Jack Prelutsky
Pictures by Victoria Chess

To the
little pigs
at
Harrisburg
School

OINK!

THE QUEEN OF EENE

Greenwillow Books

A Division of William Morrow & Company, Inc.
New York

Library of Congress Cataloging
in Publication Data

Prelutsky, Jack.
The queen of Eene
and other poems.
Summary: Fourteen humorous poems
including "Poor Old Penelope,"
"Curious Clyde," and "Uncle Bungle."
1.   Humorous poetry, American.
[1.   Humorous poetry. 2.   American
poetry] I.   Chess, Victoria.
II.   Title. PZ8.3.P9Qe 811'.5'4
77-17311   ISBN 0-688-80144-7
ISBN 0-688-84144-9 lib. bdg.

FOR REGINA,
a queen (though not of Eene)

CONTENTS

THE QUEEN OF EENE

The Queen of Eene is such a goose,
she brushed her teeth with onion juice,
and then she moaned, "I cannot see
why people do not visit me."

The Queen of Eene's the queen of dolts,
she baked a pie of nuts and bolts
and then she wondered, "Why, oh why,
does no one want to taste my pie?"

The Queen of Eene's a silly clown,
she put her crown on upside down.
"I'll turn it right side up," she said,
and so she stood upon her head.

PUMBERLY POTT'S UNPREDICTABLE NIECE

Pumberly Pott's unpredictable niece
declared with her usual zeal
that she would devour, by piece after piece,
her uncle's new automobile.

She set to her task very early one morn
by consuming the whole carburetor;
then she swallowed the windshield, the headlights and horn,
and the steering wheel just a bit later.

She chomped on the doors, on the handles and locks,
on the valves and the pistons and rings;
on the air pump and fuel pump and spark plugs and shocks,
on the brakes and the axles and springs.

When her uncle arrived she was chewing a hash
made of leftover hoses and wires
(she'd just finished eating the clutch and the dash
and the steel-belted radial tires).

"Oh what have you done to my auto," he cried,
"you strange unpredictable lass?"
"The thing wouldn't work, Uncle Pott," she replied,
  and he wept, "It was just out of gas."

ADELAIDE

Adelaide was quite dismayed;
the more she ate, the less she weighed;
the less she weighed, the more she ate,
and addled Adelaide lost weight.

She stuffed herself with meat and cheese,
potatoes, pumpkins, pies and peas,
but standing on the scale she found
that she had shed at least a pound.

She gorged herself on breasts of veal,
on roasted fish, on pickled eel,
but on completion of this feast
her scale read—ten pounds less, at least.

Poor Adelaide, that foolish glutton,
filled herself with heaps of mutton,
but when this was finally done
the scale said—minus twenty-one.

She ate until her face turned blue—
she did not know what else to do—
but when she'd finished with her plate,
she'd lost a hundred pounds of weight.

Soon Adelaide, by all accounts,
was down to hardly half an ounce,
and yet what filled her with despair
was that her cupboard shelves were bare.

For Adelaide still wished to eat—
then spied a breadcrumb by her feet;
she swiftly plucked it off the floor,
and swallowed it, then was——no more!

MISTER GAFFE

Mister Gaffe is quite peculiar
for his talking's all reversed,
he begins with what should finish,
and he ends with what comes first.

He never says, "Good morning, folks!"
the way you'd think he would,
but he tips his hat politely
and exclaims, "Folks, morning good!"

He eats breakfast in a diner
and he orders with a smile,
saying brightly to the waitress,
"Miss, please coffee some have I'll."

If he sees he has no butter
to go with his toast and cheese,
he discreetly asks his neighbor
to "butter the pass, sir, please."

If he's still a little hungry,
he will order on the side,
saying sweetly in his fashion,
"Pie apple some like I'd."

His attempts at conversation
give the local people fits.
He might talk about the weather
saying, "Today nice very it's."

In the evening, on his sofa,
he removes his shoes and tie
and to no one in particular
says, "T.V. watch I'll think I."

When he's feeling somewhat sleepy
and he see's it's his bedtime,
he yawns and says, "Late very it's
for bed to going I'm."

POOR OLD PENELOPE

Poor old Penelope,
great are her woes,
a pumpkin has started
to grow from her nose.
"My goodness," she warbles,
"this makes me so glum,
I'm perfectly certain
I planted a plum."

Poor old Penelope,
wet are her tears,
two pigeons are perched
on the lobes of her ears.
"How dreadful," she moans,
"I've such terrible luck.
I'd hoped for a goose
and a dear little duck."

Poor old Penelope,
sad is her tale,
this morning an elephant
reached her by mail.
"Oh bother," she mutters,
"I fear that I'm sunk
for all that I sent for
was one little trunk."

THE VISITOR

It came today to visit
and moved into the house,
it was smaller than an elephant
but larger than a mouse.

First it slapped my sister,
then it kicked my dad,
then it pushed my mother,
oh! that really made me mad.

It went and tickled Rover
and terrified the cat,
it sliced apart my necktie
and rudely crushed my hat.

It smeared my head with honey
and filled the tub with rocks,
and when I yelled in anger,
it stole my shoes and socks.

That's just the way it happened,
it happened all today,
before it bowed politely
and softly went away.

HERBERT GLERBETT

Herbert Glerbett, rather round,
swallowed sherbet by the pound,
fifty pounds of lemon sherbet
went inside of Herbert Glerbett.

With that glop inside his lap
Herbert Glerbett took a nap,
and as he slept, the boy dissolved,
and from the mess a thing evolved—

a thing that is a ghastly green,
a thing the world had never seen,
a puddle thing, a gooey pile
of something strange that does not smile.

Now if you're wise, and if you're sly,
you'll swiftly pass this creature by,
it is no longer Herbert Glerbett.
Whatever it is, do not disturb it.

FOUR FOOLISH LADIES

Hattie and Harriet, Hope and Hortense,
four foolish ladies without any sense,
sat for a week on a rickety fence,
Hattie and Harriet, Hope and Hortense.

Hortense and Harriet, Hattie and Hope
dressed up in envelopes, dustcloths and rope,
chewing on basketballs, swallowing soap,
Hortense and Harriet, Hattie and Hope.

Hope and Hortense, Hattie and Harriet
roped a rhinoceros using a lariat,
took him to tea in a seven-horse chariot,
Hope and Hortense, Hattie and Harriet.

Hattie and Harriet, Hope and Hortense,
four foolish ladies without any sense,
sitting once more on that rickety fence,
Hattie and Harriet, Hope and Hortense.

AUNT SAMANTHA

Aunt Samantha woke one day
and sat up in her bed,
when a middle-sized rhinoceros
sat squarely on her head.

She did not seem the least put out,
was not at all annoyed;
in fact, as she addressed the beast,
she sounded overjoyed.

"I'm very glad you're up there,
though you've squashed my head quite flat,
for you've saved me all the botherment
of putting on my hat."

THE PANCAKE COLLECTOR

Come visit my pancake collection,
it's unique in the civilized world.
I have pancakes of every description,
pancakes flaky and fluffy and curled.

I have pancakes of various sizes,
pancakes regular, heavy and light,
underdone pancakes and overdone pancakes,
and pancakes done perfectly right.

I have pancakes locked up in the closets,
I have pancakes on hangers and hooks.
They're in bags and in boxes and bureaus,
and pressed in the pages of books.

There are pretty ones sewn to the cushions
and tastefully pinned to the drapes.
The ceilings are coated with pancakes,
and the carpets are covered with crepes.

I have pancakes in most of my pockets,
and concealed in the linings of suits.
There are tiny ones stuffed in my mittens
and larger ones packed in my boots.

I have extras of most of my pancakes,
I maintain them in rows on these shelves,
and if you say nice things about them,
you may take a few home for yourselves.

I see that you've got to be going,
Won't you let yourselves out by the door?
It is time that I pour out the batter
and bake up a few hundred more.

PIGS

Pigs are stout
and pigs are kind
and pigs are seldom clean.

Snout before
and tail behind
and bacon in between.

CURIOUS CLYDE

Curious Clyde was out walking one day
when he chanced on a porcupine coming his way.
He knelt to examine the porcupine's hide—
they're still pulling quills out of Curious Clyde.

GRETCHEN IN THE KITCHEN

I see you're here to sneak some looks
at Gretchen and the way she cooks.
So peek through Gretchen's kitchen door
and watch what Gretchen has in store.

I do believe I'll boil a brew,
a wretchedly repulsive stew,
that only Gretchen can prepare.
Stop shaking! It's all right to stare.

I start with quarts of curdled mud,
and stir in spoons of dragon's blood,
then add one nose of nasty newt,
one rubber glove, one leather boot.

Then deep into my reeking vat
I toss a tongue of pickled rat,
some salted spiders (half a pound),
two candied eyeballs, sweet and round.

A lizard's gizzard, lightly mashed,
an ogre's backbone, slightly smashed,
warts of toad and scales of fish
contribute body to the dish.

Serpents' teeth and tails of mice
supply a special sort of spice
and lastly, just a pinch of paste
to season things to Gretchen's taste.

My little mix is all fixed up.
Would someone care to try a cup?
Let's hear your answers... yes or no
... now, where did everybody go?

UNCLE BUNGLE

Uncle Bungle, now deceased,
ate a cake of baker's yeast,
then with an odd gleam in his eye
consumed a large shoe-polish pie.

His dinner done, it's sad to say,
that Uncle Bungle passed away.
Uncle Bungle, now deceased,
still shines and rises in the east.